THE BIG BOOK OF
TRAINS

National Railway Museum
York, England

SCHOLASTIC CANADA LTD.

A DK Publishing Book

Editor Jane Yorke
Designer Veneta Altham
Senior Managing Editor Sarah Phillips
Senior Managing Art Editor Peter Bailey
US Editors Constance M. Robinson, Kristin Ward

DTP Designer Greg Bryant
Production Josie Alabaster
Jacket Design Andrew Nash
Picture Research James T. Robinson,
Christine Rista

Photography Mike Dunning,
Richard Leeney
National Railway Museum Consultants
Christine Heap, Stephen Hoadley, David Mosley

Published in Canada by
Scholastic Canada Ltd.,
175 Hillmount Road,
Markham,
Ontario L6C 1Z7

Canadian Cataloguing in Publication Data

Main entry under title:

The big book of trains: the biggest, fastest, longest
locomotives on rails

ISBN 0-590-03866-4

1. Locomotives – Juvenile literature. 2. Railroads –
Trains – Juvenile literature. 3. Railroads – Juvenile
literature.

TF148.B53 1998   j625.2   C98-931007-8

Color reproduction by Flying Colours, Italy
Printed and bound in Italy by Mondadori

Dorling Kindersley would like to thank *Le Shuttle*,
Calais, France, for its help with photography.

The publisher would like to thank the following for their kind
permission to reproduce their photographs:

a = above; c = center; b = below/bottom; l = left;
r = right; t = top.

Alvey & Towers: 2 ca, 3 tl, tr, 6 cl, 6-7, 8 tl, 12 tl, 25 tr, 26 c, 28;
Central Japan Railway Company: 23 tr; Colour-rail: 2 b, 10-11; Sylvia
Cordaiy Photo Library: Geoffrey Taunton 31 tl; Greater North Eastern
Railways: Fastline Photographic 24 bl; Robert Harding Picture Library:
Bildagentur Schuster/Gluske 15 tr; I. Griffiths 3 cbr, 29 tr; M. Short 29 b;
Images Colour Library: 12-13; Impact Photos: Philip Gordon 23 br;
Brian Jennison: 30 bl, 31 tr; Anthony J. Lambert: 3 car, 14 tl, 27;
Richard Leeney: 19 tr; Milepost 92¹/₂: 19 br; Brian Lovell 3 bl, 22-23;
National Railway Museum, York: 4 c; NPS Photo: Ken Ganz 10 tl;
Photo Affairs Bildarchiv: Jürgen Bögelspacher 3 cbl, 20 tr, 20-21, 21 tr,
26 b, 29 tl; QA Photos: 3 cl, 16 bl, 18-19; Quadrant Picture Library:
Railway Gazette 21 cr; Science Museum: 2 t, 4 bl, 4-5, 7 tr; South
American Pictures: Tony Morrison 26 t; Spectrum Colour Library:
D. & J. Heaton 22 tr; Swedish State Railways: Industrifotografen AB
24-25; Telegraph Colour Library: Bildagentur 24 cl; Jim Winkley: 3 cal,
br, 9 tl, tr, 12 bl, 14-15, 30-31; Mike Bledsoe 11 t.

Jacket: Images Colour Library: front; Milepost 92¹/₂: Brian Soloman
back tr, spine b; QA Photos: back b; Telegraph Colour Library: Japack
Photo Library spine a.

Early steam locomotives   4

American steam locomotives   6

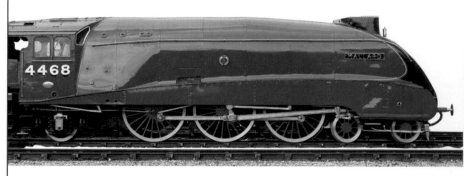

Fast steam locomotives   8

Powerful
steam locomotives   10

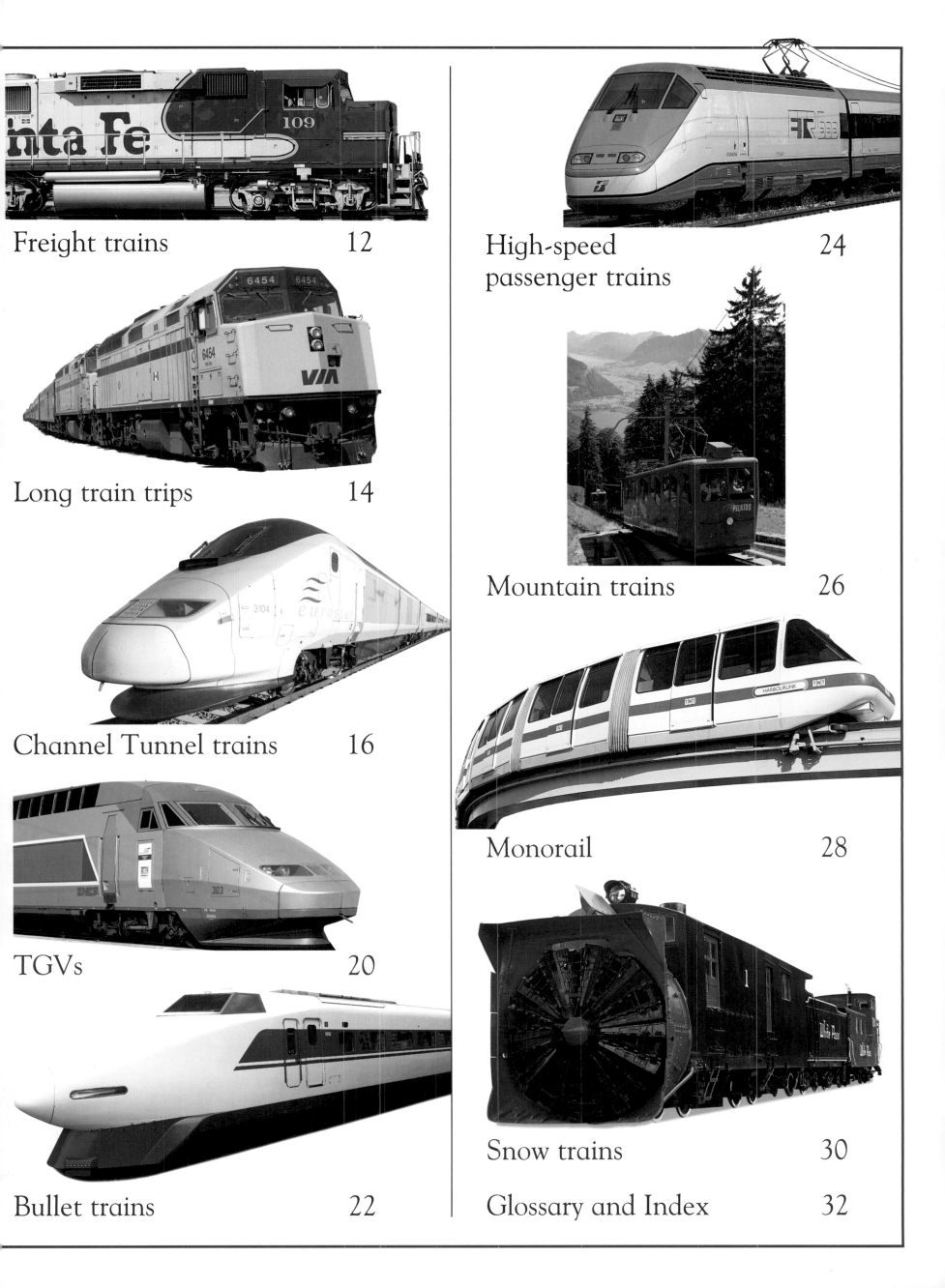

Freight trains 12

Long train trips 14

Channel Tunnel trains 16

TGVs 20

Bullet trains 22

High-speed passenger trains 24

Mountain trains 26

Monorail 28

Snow trains 30

Glossary and Index 32

Early steam locomotives

In Britain, the first railroads were built to carry coal, and horses were used to pull the open freight cars along. In 1804, Richard Trevithick built the first steam locomotive, but it was slower than a horse and so heavy that it kept breaking the track. Soon people were making reliable steam locomotives that could carry goods and passengers quickly over longer distances.

This cutaway replica of Rocket enables you to see inside the boiler.

The tender carried coke for fuel. Water was carried in the barrel.

First-class passenger cars were similar to stagecoaches.

First railroad

Rocket worked on the Liverpool and Manchester Railway, opened in 1830. This was the first railroad to provide passenger trains pulled by steam locomotives.

Rocket locomotive

Rocket was designed by Briton Robert Stephenson in 1829. This 5-ton (4.5-tonne) steam locomotive was successful because the design used all the latest ideas. It could travel at speeds of up to 25 miles (40 kilometers) per hour on its intercity journey.

Exhaust steam went up the tall chimney.

The boiler heated water to make steam.

The steam pushed the pistons and the connecting rods turned the wheels.

The fireman shoveled coke into the firebox. The heat from the fire passed along tubes inside the boiler.

The driver and fireman stood on a small platform.

The huge cylinders containing the pistons were upright on this engine.

Puffing Billy took its name from the loud noise made by the exhaust steam.

Transporting coal

Puffing Billy is one of the oldest surviving steam locomotives. It was built in England in 1813, to a design by William Hedley. The locomotive worked for 48 years on a railroad just 5 miles (8 kilometers) long. It pulled coal cars at walking pace from Wylam coal mine to a nearby river for transportation by barge.

The pistons made the beams rock backward and forward. These moved the connecting rods, which turned the wheels.

The boiler produced steam, which entered the cylinders and pushed the pistons.

The tender carried the coke fuel supply.

The locomotive ran on cast-iron, "fish-bellied" rails. These had a thicker midsection for added strength.

The connecting rods moved cogs, which turned the wheels.

American steam locomotives

Railroads soon spread all over the world, carrying people and goods faster than anything else had before. The first railroad built across the United States was finished in May 1869. Colorful steam locomotives, like the ones shown here, carried settlers traveling to the new towns in the west. These locomotives were called 4-4-0s, because they had four driving wheels and four bogie wheels to guide the engine on the sometimes poor track. The bogie could swivel from side to side around the twisting tracks.

The chimney let out smoke and used steam.

A large, powerful oil lamp warned people that a train was coming at night.

119

Door into the smoke box

The cowcatcher was a strong, metal grid for pushing wandering buffalo off the track.

Wood-burning locomotive

Jupiter was an early American locomotive that burned wood for fuel. This famous engine worked on the Central Pacific Railroad. It had a large funnel-shaped chimney to catch the shower of sparks that came out of the engine with the smoke and steam.

Coal-burning locomotive

By 1875, some American steam locomotives were using coal for fuel. This model shows how much of the pipework was on the outside for easy maintenance.

Warning bell

Tender

Four driving wheels

Four-wheeled bogie

Cowcatcher

The sand box sprinkled sand onto wet rails to give the wheels more grip.

The steam whistle used to warn people and animals of the train's approach.

The boiler turned the water into steam.

The firebox burned the coal to heat the water.

Heading out west

Locomotive 119 traveled westward across America on the Union Pacific Railroad. The engine weighed 40 tons (36 tonnes) and could pull about six passenger cars. At full steam, it could speed along at 50 miles (80 kilometers) per hour.

A large cab protected the driver and fireman from the wind and weather.

The tender carried 5 tons (4 tonnes) of coal and 2,400 gallons (9,000 liters) of water to power the train for 93 miles (150 kilometers).

The steam pushed the piston, which moved the connecting rod and turned the wheels.

Fast steam locomotives

Large cylinders make the engine very powerful.

The casing opens up for cleaning the inside of the engine.

No 4498
CLASS A4

Some passenger trains, called express trains, are designed to run nonstop between two cities. In the 1930s, the finest steam locomotives ever built pulled such trains. Some had sleek, streamlined shapes to help them go faster, and bigger engines that could run for long periods at over 99 miles (160 kilometers) per hour.

Locomotive engineer

This locomotive is an A4 Class, the same type as *Mallard*. It is named *Sir Nigel Gresley*, after the mechanical engineer who designed the engines.

Fastest steam locomotive

Mallard holds the unbeaten record as the fastest steam locomotive in the world. On July 3, 1938, it reached a speed of 125 miles (202 kilometers) per hour running downhill between Grantham and Peterborough, in England. This record was set during brake equipment trials on the streamlined cars of the London and North Eastern Railway.

4468

The driver and fireman operated the locomotive from the foot plate.

These rods drove a very accurate speedometer.

This plaque commemorates Mallard's *record-breaking run in 1938*.

The smoke box door can be opened to clean the soot out of the front of the engine.

The locomotive number is painted on the front of the engine.

Famous express train

Flying Scotsman is one of the most famous locomotives in the world. In 1928, it headed the first nonstop express train from London to Edinburgh, in Scotland, a distance of 413 miles (665 kilometers). On its daily run in 1934, the steam locomotive set a speed record of 100 miles (161 kilometers) per hour.

Train attraction

Flying Scotsman is still kept in working order today, so that passengers can enjoy traveling on a train pulled by this very famous locomotive.

Mallard *can be seen on display at the National Railway Museum in York.*

The specially designed double chimney let out steam and smoke.

The streamlined nose and engine casing helped the locomotive travel at high speeds.

The 181-ton (165-tonne) engine was over 69 feet (21 meters) long.

Mallard *was a 4-6-2 locomotive. It had 4 leading wheels, 6 big 7-foot (2-meter) driving wheels, and 2 trailing wheels.*

Powerful steam locomotives

By the 1940s, engineers were designing bigger and more powerful steam engines to pull heavy freight trains at higher speeds. These huge locomotives often had two sets of cylinders and driving wheels under one very large boiler. They were called articulated engines because the driving wheels could pivot under the boiler to travel around tight curves.

254 tons
(230 tonnes)

Biggest steam locomotive

America's Union Pacific Railroad had 25 *Big Boy* locomotives built between 1941 and 1944, based on an idea by Anatole Mallet. The huge engines – 131 feet (40 meters) long, 16 feet (5 meters) high – had 16 driving wheels and could go 81 miles (130 kilometers) per hour.

The large boiler supplied steam to the two power units.

The bunker held 28 tons (25 tonnes) of coal.

African freight

From 1954, the 20A Class Garratt locomotive hauled loads of coal and copper in the countries now called Zambia and Zimbabwe. This articulated locomotive had engine units at the front and back, with the boiler slung between them. The design enabled the powerful locomotive to travel around curves on light track in the African bush.

The front engine unit had 4 leading wheels, 8 driving wheels, and 2 trailing wheels.

The driver had a poor view down the length of the huge boiler.

This 4-6-6-4 locomotive had six front driving wheels, powered by a set of cylinders.

The heavy engine could pull 1,543 tons (1,400 tonnes) of freight.

American giant

The Challenger was the *Big Boy*'s little cousin, being only 121 feet (37 meters) long. The engine had 12 driving wheels and was used to haul trains carrying passengers and goods over the Rocky Mountains and across the western deserts.

The cowcatcher prevented animals on the track from derailing the locomotive.

Water for the boiler was carried in this tank at the front of the engine.

The brake pipes ran the entire length of the train and enabled the driver to control all of the train vehicles.

Freight trains

Today's cleaner, diesel-electric locomotives have replaced the powerful steam locomotives of the past. These modern engines are able to haul large amounts of freight over long distances using less fuel than trucks would need. They transport all sorts of goods: food produce like wheat and eggs, coal for industry, cars, and even tanks!

The locomotive runs at a top speed of 62 miles (100 kilometers) per hour.

Long-haul journeys

The Santa Fe diesel-electric locomotive is used to haul freight over 2,000 miles (3,541 kilometers) across the United States, from California to Chicago. The large fuel tanks keep the engines going on the long desert runs.

Huge tanks carry up to 462 gallons (1,750 liters) of diesel fuel.

The driver enters the cab using the steps and a door in the front of the locomotive.

The air brakes act directly on the wheels to stop the train safely.

Pulling power

This heavy freight train crossing the deserts of Arizona is hauled by five diesel engines, operated by just one driver. The whole train is almost 1.5 miles (2 kilometers) long. Behind the locomotives, there are five double-decker freight cars. The following 80 or more cars carry freight in large containers, loaded in a "piggy-back" fashion.

The small snowplow can clear snowdrifts or debris off the line.

The driver's cab is fully protected against the weather.

Locomotive identification number

Powerful freight locomotive

This freight locomotive of the Santa Fe Railroad is 49 feet (15 meters) long and weighs 123 tons (112 tonnes). Diesel oil fuels the engine that generates electricity to drive the wheels.

8270

The 12 driving wheels are powered by electric motors.

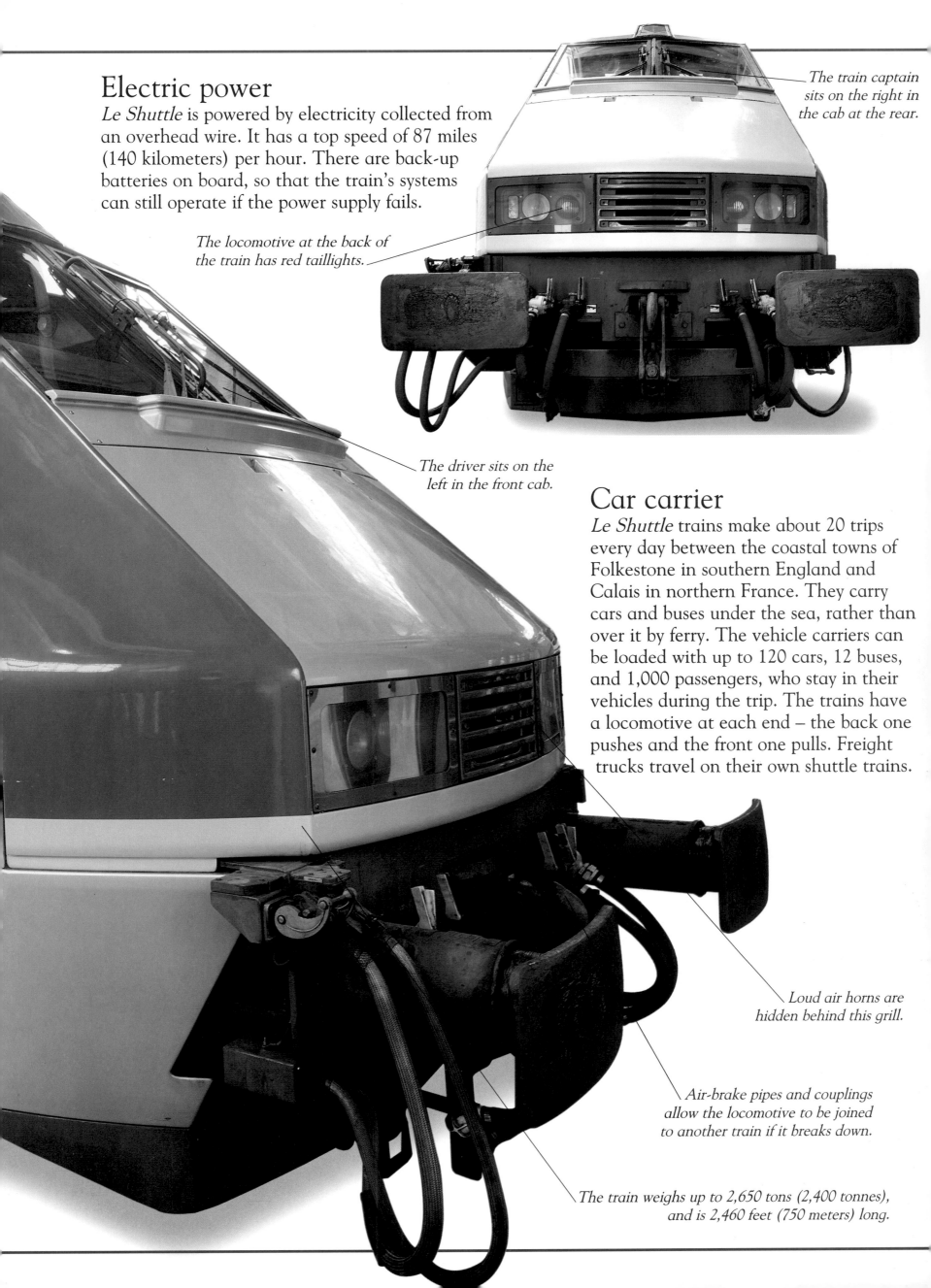

Electric power

Le Shuttle is powered by electricity collected from an overhead wire. It has a top speed of 87 miles (140 kilometers) per hour. There are back-up batteries on board, so that the train's systems can still operate if the power supply fails.

The train captain sits on the right in the cab at the rear.

The locomotive at the back of the train has red taillights.

The driver sits on the left in the front cab.

Car carrier

Le Shuttle trains make about 20 trips every day between the coastal towns of Folkestone in southern England and Calais in northern France. They carry cars and buses under the sea, rather than over it by ferry. The vehicle carriers can be loaded with up to 120 cars, 12 buses, and 1,000 passengers, who stay in their vehicles during the trip. The trains have a locomotive at each end – the back one pushes and the front one pulls. Freight trucks travel on their own shuttle trains.

Loud air horns are hidden behind this grill.

Air-brake pipes and couplings allow the locomotive to be joined to another train if it breaks down.

The train weighs up to 2,650 tons (2,400 tonnes), and is 2,460 feet (750 meters) long.

Channel Tunnel trains

The Channel Tunnel is 31 miles (50 kilometers) long and runs under the English Channel, linking the railroads of France and England. Special electric trains have been running through the tunnel since 1994. *Le Shuttle* is the service that transports cars and trucks. High-speed *Eurostar* trains carry passengers between London, Paris, and Brussels.

Springs help insure a more comfortable ride.

Underwater journey

The Channel Tunnel trip takes about 30 minutes. There are actually three tunnels dug 150 feet (45 meters) below the seabed. Trains run in opposite directions in the two large tunnels on either side of a smaller, safety-access tunnel.

Sand carried in this box is blown onto the rails to give the wheels more traction in wet weather.

Long train trips

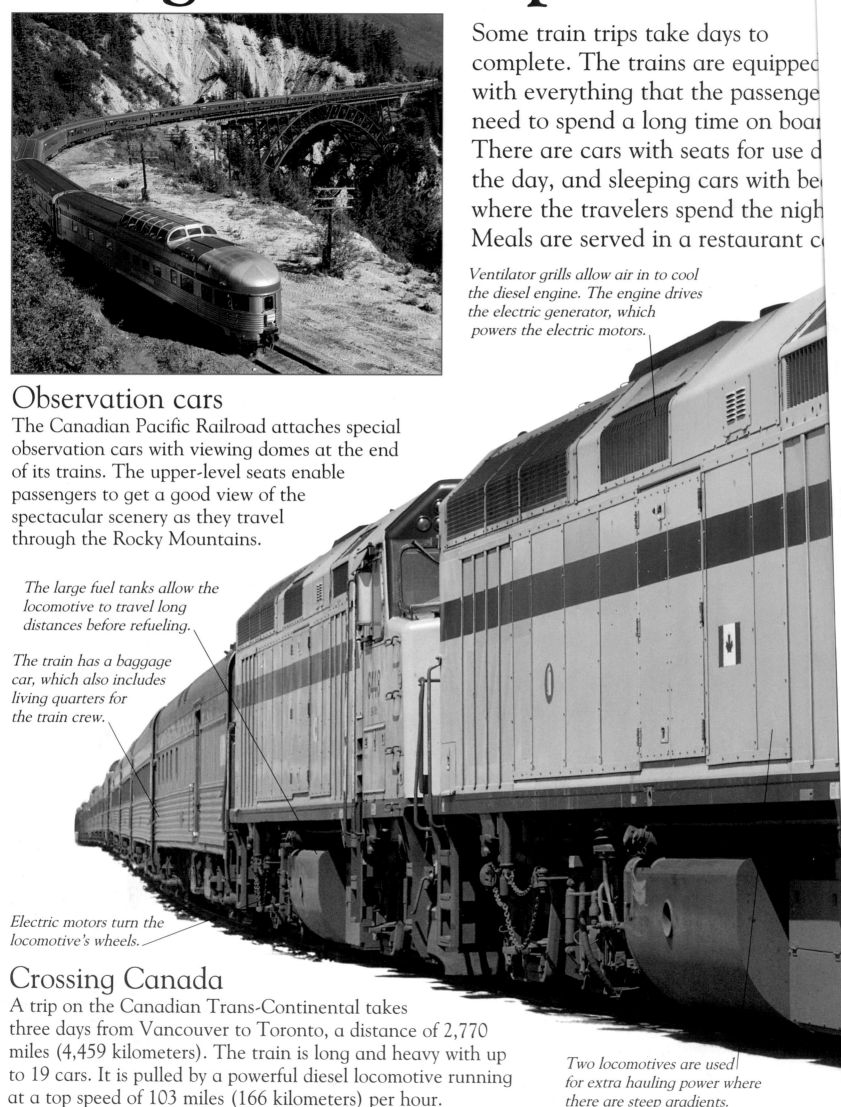

Some train trips take days to complete. The trains are equipped with everything that the passengers need to spend a long time on board. There are cars with seats for use during the day, and sleeping cars with beds where the travelers spend the night. Meals are served in a restaurant car.

Ventilator grills allow air in to cool the diesel engine. The engine drives the electric generator, which powers the electric motors.

Observation cars

The Canadian Pacific Railroad attaches special observation cars with viewing domes at the end of its trains. The upper-level seats enable passengers to get a good view of the spectacular scenery as they travel through the Rocky Mountains.

The large fuel tanks allow the locomotive to travel long distances before refueling.

The train has a baggage car, which also includes living quarters for the train crew.

Electric motors turn the locomotive's wheels.

Crossing Canada

A trip on the Canadian Trans-Continental takes three days from Vancouver to Toronto, a distance of 2,770 miles (4,459 kilometers). The train is long and heavy with up to 19 cars. It is pulled by a powerful diesel locomotive running at a top speed of 103 miles (166 kilometers) per hour.

Two locomotives are used for extra hauling power where there are steep gradients.

TGVs

The *Train à Grande Vitesse,* or TGV, is France's high-speed electric train. It came into service in 1981, running from Paris to Lyon. In 1990, an improved TGV *Atlantique* linked Paris and Bordeaux. The TGV travels along specially constructed tracks at up to 190 miles (300 kilometers) per hour.

Locomotives at both ends

All TGVs have a powerful electric motor unit, or engine, attached to the front and back of the train.

The locomotive's eight driving wheels are powered by electric motors.

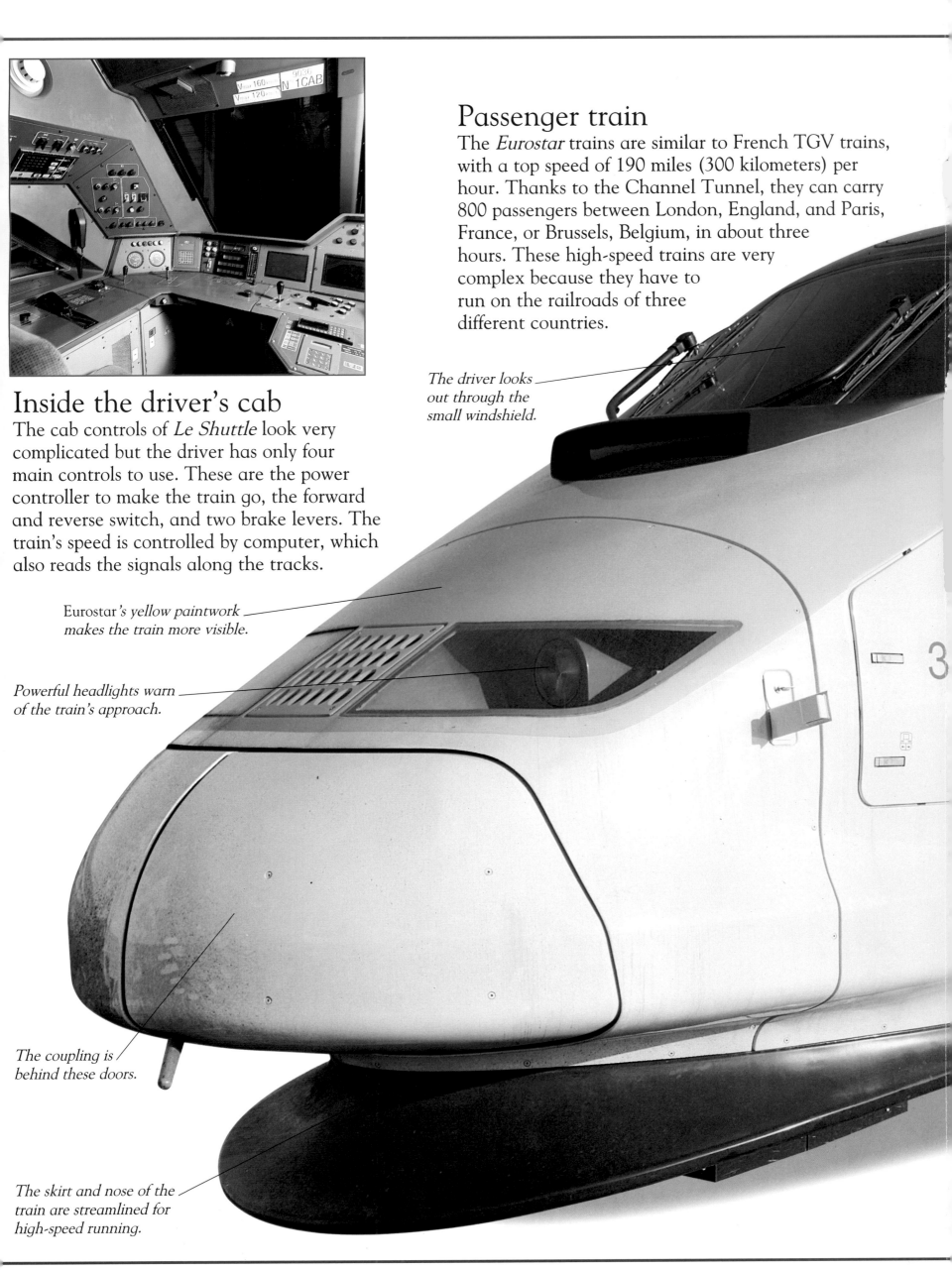

Passenger train

The *Eurostar* trains are similar to French TGV trains, with a top speed of 190 miles (300 kilometers) per hour. Thanks to the Channel Tunnel, they can carry 800 passengers between London, England, and Paris, France, or Brussels, Belgium, in about three hours. These high-speed trains are very complex because they have to run on the railroads of three different countries.

The driver looks out through the small windshield.

Inside the driver's cab

The cab controls of *Le Shuttle* look very complicated but the driver has only four main controls to use. These are the power controller to make the train go, the forward and reverse switch, and two brake levers. The train's speed is controlled by computer, which also reads the signals along the tracks.

Eurostar's yellow paintwork makes the train more visible.

Powerful headlights warn of the train's approach.

The coupling is behind these doors.

The skirt and nose of the train are streamlined for high-speed running.

Waterloo station

Eurostar trains have their own specially built platforms at Waterloo Station, in London. Just like at airports, international passengers go through passport checks before catching their trains.

Ventilator grills let in air to cool down the electrical equipment.

Passengers can buy refreshments from the on-board buffet service.

Eurostar is 1,115 feet (340 meters) long. It has 20 passenger cars and a locomotive at each end.

Eurostar in Britain

In France and Belgium, *Eurostar* travels on special high-speed lines. In Britain, the trains are slower, because they share the same tracks as ordinary trains.

The train gathers electricity from the overhead wire with its pantograph, or from a third rail on the ground with this special pickup.

Longest train trip

It takes eight days to travel on the Trans-Siberian Express from Moscow to Vladivostok in the Russian Federation. The line is 5,765 miles (9,279 kilometers) long, and the train stops at 70 stations along the way. This makes it the longest train trip in the world without changing trains.

The driver climbs up steps into the driving cab. From here, he gets a good view of the line ahead.

On some parts of the line, the Trans-Siberian Express runs on electricity picked up from an overhead wire.

The strong headlights let people see the train coming.

6454

6454

6454

GPA-30c

VIA

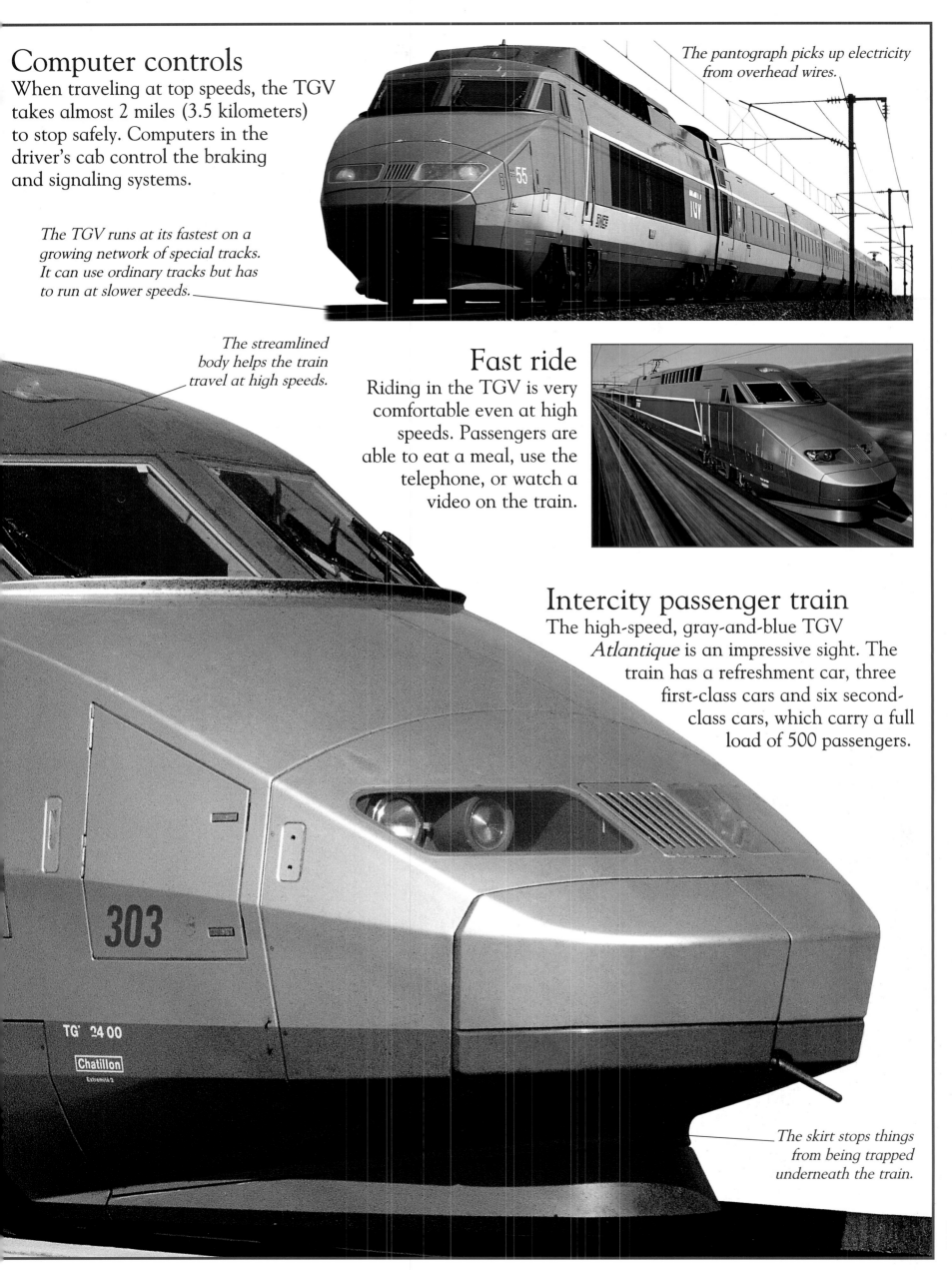

Computer controls

When traveling at top speeds, the TGV takes almost 2 miles (3.5 kilometers) to stop safely. Computers in the driver's cab control the braking and signaling systems.

The pantograph picks up electricity from overhead wires.

The TGV runs at its fastest on a growing network of special tracks. It can use ordinary tracks but has to run at slower speeds.

The streamlined body helps the train travel at high speeds.

Fast ride

Riding in the TGV is very comfortable even at high speeds. Passengers are able to eat a meal, use the telephone, or watch a video on the train.

Intercity passenger train

The high-speed, gray-and-blue TGV *Atlantique* is an impressive sight. The train has a refreshment car, three first-class cars and six second-class cars, which carry a full load of 500 passengers.

The skirt stops things from being trapped underneath the train.

303

TG 2400

Chatillon
Extremité 2

Bullet trains

The futuristic-looking, high-speed electric trains that run in Japan are called Bullet trains. Their Japanese name is *Shinkansen*. First introduced in 1964, the trains provided the first passenger service in the world to travel at speeds of 100 miles (161 kilometers) per hour. Today, the trains reach much faster speeds of up to 190 miles (300 kilometers) per hour, running on specially designed tracks. Bullet trains also offer very frequent service, and carry nearly one million passengers a day.

Speeding past Mount Fuji
This modern type of Bullet train is made of aluminum alloy for lightness and speed.

High-speed journey
The Series 100 Bullet train has a top speed of 141 miles (228 kilometers) per hour. It has cut the intercity time from Tokyo to Osaka, a distance of 321 miles (516 kilometers), to three hours.

The driver sits high up and has a clear view of the line ahead.

The powerful headlight also acts as a red taillight when the train is traveling the other way.

This brush sweeps small stones and debris off the rail, away from the train wheels.

The streamlined nose looks very similar to an airplane.

Train of the future

This unusual-looking train, currently in development, has no wheels. It is called a Maglev, which is short for "magnetic levitation." Strong magnets on the bottom of the train and on the track raise the train slightly off the ground, and a powerful magnetic field moves the train along. The reduced friction means that the train can travel as fast as 341 miles (550 kilometers) per hour.

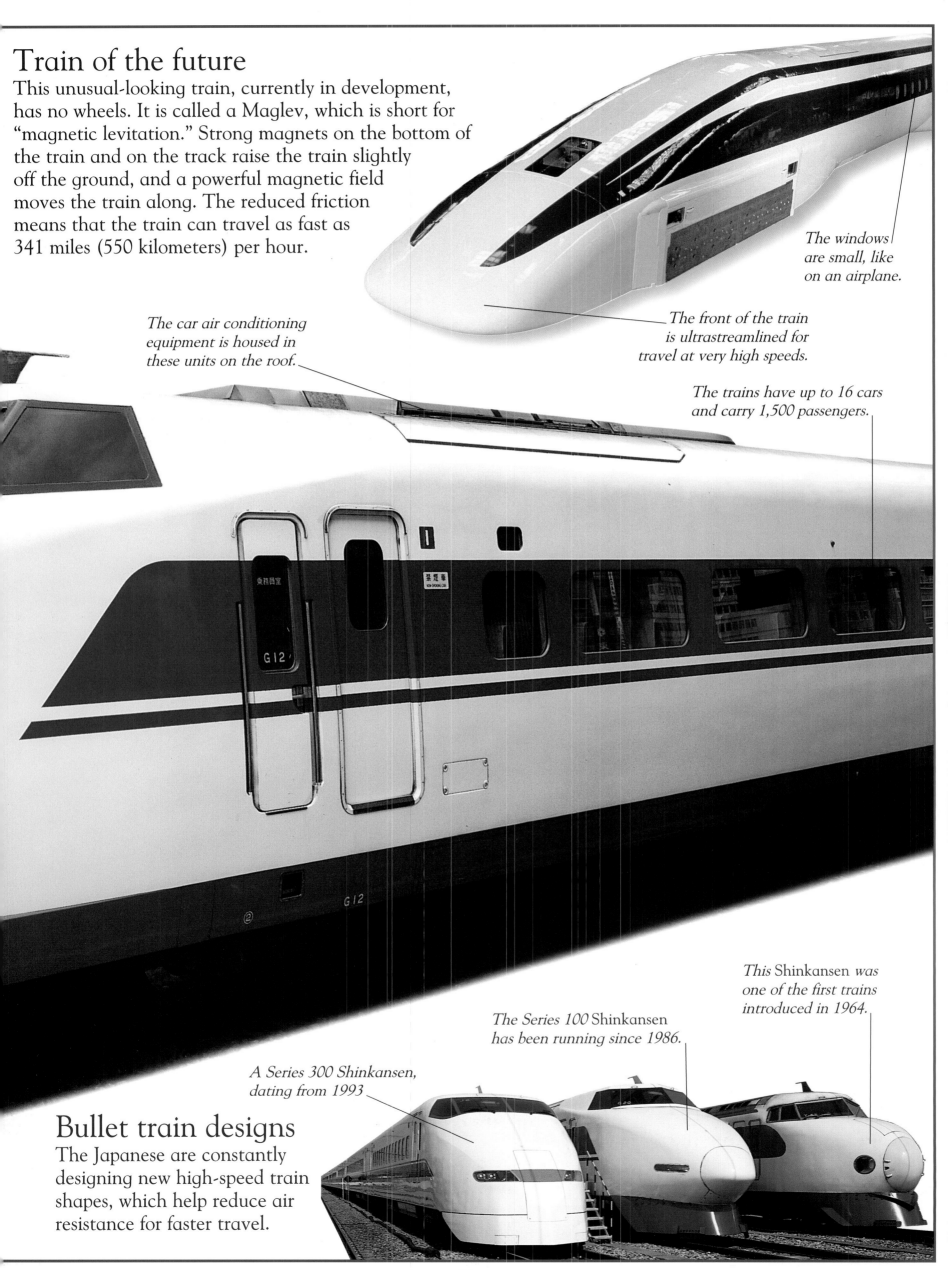

The windows are small, like on an airplane.

The car air conditioning equipment is housed in these units on the roof.

The front of the train is ultrastreamlined for travel at very high speeds.

The trains have up to 16 cars and carry 1,500 passengers.

This Shinkansen was one of the first trains introduced in 1964.

The Series 100 Shinkansen has been running since 1986.

A Series 300 Shinkansen, dating from 1993

Bullet train designs

The Japanese are constantly designing new high-speed train shapes, which help reduce air resistance for faster travel.

High-speed passenger trains

Electric trains are now running at faster and faster speeds, because they have to compete with cars and airplanes for passengers traveling between major cities. High-speed passenger trains run on electric power picked up from overhead lines. Some countries have built brand-new railroad networks for their fast electric trains. Others run a high-speed service on existing tracks and fit the trains into their normal schedules.

The train has a driving car at both ends, which makes it possible to depart right away on the return trip.

Headlights or taillights are used, depending on which way the train is traveling.

Fast and slow tracks

Germany's high-speed trains run on both existing tracks and newly built lines. The ICE electric engines can run only at their top speed of 174 miles (280 kilometers) per hour when traveling on the new lines.

The lip on the power car acts as a small snowplow.

The driving trailer has space for carrying baggage.

England to Scotland

The GNER 225 has a top speed of 140 miles (225 kilometers) per hour. It runs between London and Edinburgh on Britain's Great North Eastern Railway.

Traveling on straight lines

The new Italian ETR 500 can travel at 190 miles (300 kilometers) per hour. It runs on specially built high-speed routes with few curves. This means that the train can maintain its fast speed without slowing down for curves or other traffic on the line.

The pantograph picks up electric power from overhead wires.

Tilting train

The railroads of Sweden are all twists and turns. The engine and cars of the X2000 train tilt when going around corners. This enables the train to keep up its top speed of 125 miles (200 kilometers) per hour.

The X2000 power car pulls five passenger cars on its intercity trips.

Mountain trains

Railroads are very popular in mountainous areas where it would be difficult to build a road. Many mountain railroads were built just so that people could enjoy the view from the train. Rack railroads have special tracks that can run up the sides of mountains. The train has a powered cogwheel under the engine, which grips a toothed rail. This allows the train to climb very steep slopes and prevents it from slipping backward.

World's highest railroad
The Huancayo-Huancay line in Peru is the world's highest railroad. This ordinary railroad reaches a height of 15,846 feet (4,830 meters). The steam locomotives that run here were built in England.

Tourist train
The Brienz Rothorn train is now just a tourist attraction. This rack railroad is 5 miles (7.5 kilometers) long and is the only one in Switzerland that still uses steam locomotives. Powerful engines push the passenger cars up the mountainside, to a height of 5,511 feet (1,680 meters).

The passenger car is pushed uphill by the steam locomotive.

A cogged wheel on the engine climbs up the toothed rack.

The locomotive is built at an angle so that it stays level on the steep slope.

Bridges and tunnels
Railroads in mountainous areas have to use many bridges, viaducts, and tunnels to pass through difficult terrain. This train is called the *Glacier Express* because it runs through deep snow for many months of the year. It carries passengers to ski resorts in the Swiss mountains.

Steepest rack railroad

The Mount Pilatus Railroad in Switzerland is the steepest rack railroad in the world. The railroad used steam engines when it was opened in 1889, but electric trains took over in 1937. The trains are single cars and have a top speed of 6 miles (9 kilometers) per hour.

The pantograph collects electricity from the wires running overhead.

The cars are specially designed so that the passenger seats match the angle of the slope.

Some sections of the track slide sideways to enable trains to pass each other.

Trains travel up and down the mountain on the same track.

The rack is laid between the ordinary rails.

Hanging train

The Wuppertal monorail, in Germany, is built over a river. The hanging cars are like an ordinary train, but the driving wheels are on the roof.

The train is powered by electric motors.

Tracks run in both directions.

Giant steel legs support the monorail track.

The stations are at the same level as the track. Passengers reach the platforms by escalator.

Monorail

These special trains hang or balance on a single rail, called a monorail. The trains have motors, which are powered by electricity. Monorail trains run high up off the ground and carry passengers across busy cities, traveling over the tops of roads, buildings, and even rivers! Riding on a monorail seems like flying and can be very exciting.

Streamlined train

The Sydney Harbourlink monorail, in Australia, is streamlined. The driver's cab has a sloping windshield, so it looks very futuristic. However the train travels quite slowly at about 17 miles (30 kilometers) per hour.

Avoiding the busy traffic

People use the monorail like a bus to travel short distances to work, or to the stores. Some children even go to school on it.

Ribbed panels enable the cars to travel around tight bends.

Rubber side wheels guide the train safely along the metal track.

The windshield wiper helps the driver have a clear view ahead.

Monorails for fun

Some monorails, like the Seattle Expo Alweg, in Washington State, are built to take visitors around a large exhibition or amusement park. The cars have big windows so everyone can see out and get a good view.
Monorails usually have only one or two cars, which can carry up to 100 people.

Sliding doors let the passengers in and out at stations.

The train cars straddle the concrete track.

The wheels run along the top of the rail and carry the train's weight. Guide wheels run along the sides to keep the train balanced.

Snow trains

When railroad tracks become blocked by snow, special trains are needed to dig out the tracks so that trains can start running again. Snowplows can be used to clear deep snowdrifts, but in really severe conditions, rotary snowblowers are needed to open up the tracks. These snow trains were first used in the United States in 1869.

Loose snow was broken up by the wheel, blown out of this chute, and thrown clear of the track.

The powerful headlight could light up the track in blizzard conditions.

Large side blades sliced a path through the snowdrifts and channeled the snow into the spinning wheel.

The giant spinning wheel broke up the snow.

The snowblower was powered by steam from a boiler inside the blower.

Clearing tracks
Snowblowers clear the tracks before other trains start running. In very heavy snow storms, they may be needed to rescue stranded trains.

Diesel power

This British snow train is diesel-powered and does not need a locomotive to push it. Large blades break up the snow, which is then blown clear of the track. Deep snow is rare in Britain, so the train is stored in a depot when not in use.

Snowblower at work

This steam-powered snowblower clears the tracks by cutting into the snowdrift and then blowing the loose snow away from the tracks. The train can clear about 131 feet (40 meters) of deep snow per minute and is moved along the tracks by "pusher" locomotives.

The tender carried the coal and water to fuel the boiler.

This vehicle contained equipment and facilities for the crew.

White Pass

White Pass

Steam snowblower

This snowblower worked on the railroads of Alaska, and was powered by steam. It had a crew of three: the fireman, the engineer who took care of the machinery, and the pilot who signaled to the "pusher" locomotives.

Glossary

Bogie
A set of four wheels fitted under a locomotive or freight car to help it turn on curved track.

Boiler
The large metal drum on a steam locomotive, where the water is turned into steam.

Car
The coaches that carry passengers on a train.

Coke
A type of coal used as fuel for early steam locomotives.

Connecting rod
A metal rod that links the piston to the driving wheels of a steam locomotive.

Coupling
A device for joining cars to an engine and to each other to form a train.

Coupling rod
The metal rod that links a pair of driving wheels together.

Cylinder
The metal tube in which steam or gas under pressure pushes the piston to drive the wheels.

Diesel-electric engine
A locomotive using diesel oil as the fuel to generate electricity, which in turn powers electric motors that drive the wheels.

Driving wheels
The main wheels that are connected to a power supply and move a locomotive.

Electric engine
A locomotive powered by electricity picked up from an electric cable or third rail.

Firebox
The metal box behind a steam locomotive's boiler, where the fuel is burned.

Fireman
The person on a steam engine who shovels coal into the firebox and keeps the boiler filled with water.

Foot plate
The driver's cab on a steam engine.

Freight car
A train vehicle that carries freight, or goods.

Locomotive
The vehicle that provides the power to move a train.

Pantograph
A metal frame on top of an electric locomotive that picks up electricity from cables hanging above the track.

Piston rod
The moving rod inside a cylinder that helps to turn a locomotive's driving wheels.

Power car
A diesel or electric locomotive permanently joined to a set of passenger carriages.

Third rail
A rail on the ground that supplies electricity to some electric trains.

Index of trains

Big Boy 10
Brienz Rothorn train 26
Bullet train 22, 23

Canadian Trans-Continental 14
Challenger 11

ETR 500 25
Eurostar 16, 18, 19

Flying Scotsman 9

Garratt 10, 11
Glacier Express 26
GNER 225 24

Huancayo to Huancay train 26

ICE 24

Jupiter 6

Locomotive 119 6, 7

Maglev 23
Mallard 8, 9
Mount Pilatus train 27

Puffing Billy 5

Rocket 4

Santa Fe freight train 12, 13
Seattle Expo Alweg monorail 29
Le Shuttle 16, 17, 18
Sir Nigel Gresley 8
snowblower 30, 31
Sydney Harbourlink monorail 29

TGV 18, 20, 21
Trans-Siberian Express 15

Wuppertal monorail 28

X2000 24, 25